REMARKABLE

PEOPLE

Prince William and Kate Middleton

by Lauren Diemer
and Heather Kissock

MEDIA ENHANCED BOOKS
AV2 BY WEIGL
ADDED VALUE · AUDIO VISUAL

www.av2books.com

AV² provides enriched content that supplements and complements this book. Weigl's AV² books strive to create inspired learning and engage young minds in a total learning experience.

Your AV² Media Enhanced books come alive with...

Audio
Listen to sections of the book read aloud.

Key Words
Study vocabulary, and complete a matching word activity.

Video
Watch informative video clips.

Quizzes
Test your knowledge.

Embedded Weblinks
Gain additional information for research.

Slide Show
View images and captions, and prepare a presentation.

Try This!
Complete activities and hands-on experiments.

... and much, much more!

Go to **www.av2books.com**, and enter this book's unique code.

BOOK CODE

F483895

AV² by Weigl brings you media enhanced books that support active learning.

Published by AV² by Weigl
350 5th Avenue, 59th Floor
New York, NY 10118

www.av2books.com   www.weigl.com

Library of Congress Cataloging-in-Publication Data

Diemer, Lauren.
 Prince William and Kate Middleton / Lauren Diemer and Heather Kissock.
   pages cm. -- (Remarkable people)
 Includes index.
 Summary: "Explores the life and times of Prince William and Kate Middleton, providing an in-depth look at the inspiration, achievements, and successes that define them. Intended for fourth to sixth grade students"--Provided by publisher.
 ISBN 978-1-62127-392-9 (hardcover : alk. paper) -- ISBN 978-1-62127-398-1 (softcover : alk. paper)
 1. William, Prince, Duke of Cambridge, 1982---Juvenile literature. 2. Catherine, Duchess of Cambridge, 1982---Juvenile literature. 3. Royal couples--Great Britain--Biography--Juvenile literature. 4. Princes--Great Britain--Biography--Juvenile literature. 5. Princesses--Great Britain--Biography--Juvenile literature. I. Kissock, Heather. II. Title.
 DA591.A45 W55527
 941.086092'2--dc23
 [B]
                        2013000837

Printed in the United States of America in North Mankato, Minnesota
2 3 4 5 6 7 8 9 0 17 16 15 14

012014
WEP270114

Editor: Heather Kissock
Design: Terry Paulhus

Photograph Credits
Weigl acknowledges Getty Images as the primary image supplier for this title.
Every reasonable effort has been made to trace ownership and to obtain permission to reprint copyright material. The publishers would be pleased to have any errors or omissions brought to their attention so that they may be corrected in subsequent printings.

Contents

Who Are Prince William and Kate Middleton?

On April 29, 2011, more than 300 million people worldwide turned on their televisions to watch England's Prince William marry Kate Middleton. The couple is now known as the Duke and Duchess of Cambridge. One day, they will become the king and queen of the **United Kingdom**.

> *"My guiding principles in life are to be honest, genuine, thoughtful and caring."*
> *– Prince William*

To prepare for their future role, the couple has already begun taking on royal duties. They have embarked on several tours to other continents and countries. The couple has also become active in supporting many charities and organizations. They often appear in public to promote causes that are important to them, their families, and the country. In doing this, William and Kate represent the United Kingdom to the rest of the world.

What attracts most people to William and Kate is their down-to-earth ways. Both are determined to keep their lives as normal as possible. William has a full-time job as a helicopter pilot with the Royal Air Force. Kate looks after their household. Their casual approach to being royal has earned the couple many fans.

Growing Up

Prince William Arthur Philip Louis Windsor was born on June 21, 1982, in London, England. William is the son of Prince Charles and his first wife, Diana. Prince Charles is the current **heir** to the British crown. Two years after William was born, the prince and princess had another son. They named him Henry. Today, he is better known as Prince Harry.

Catherine Elizabeth Middleton, or Kate, was born on January 9, 1982, in Reading, a small town in south-central England. Her father, Michael, and her mother, Carole, both worked for an airline. Kate is the oldest of three children. She has a sister, Philippa, and a brother, James.

Even though Kate and William did not meet until they were older, they shared many similar interests as children. Both were very athletic. William was the captain of his swim team. Kate played tennis and field hockey. The two also shared an interest in the arts. They sang at school concerts and acted in school plays.

■ As a baby, Prince William lived with his parents in London's Kensington Palace.

Get to Know England

FLOWER
Rose

FLAG

ANIMAL
Lion

London is the capital city of England. It is home to Buckingham Palace, an official residence of Queen Elizabeth II, William's grandmother.

England's kings and queens are crowned in Westminster Abbey, a large church in central London.

In 1215, King John of England signed the Magna Carta at Runnymede. This document is considered the foundation of **democracy** in the modern world.

The Royal Family sometimes stays at Windsor Castle. It is the oldest and largest royal residence still in use anywhere in the world.

Think about it!

Being a member of a royal family can seem glamorous. However, royalty has many responsibilities and is constantly in the public eye. What do you think would be the best part about being royal? What would be the worst part? Would you want to grow up knowing that you would someday be king or queen of a country? How would knowing this affect the way you live your life?

Practice Makes Perfect

Whthen William and Kate finished their regular schooling, both took a **gap year** before going to university. William spent his gap year doing **volunteer** work in England, Africa, and Chile. He also participated in military exercises in Belize. Kate spent her gap year taking classes in Italy and working as a crewmember on a racing boat. Like William, she also volunteered in Chile.

By 2001, both were ready to begin university. Each was accepted into the University of St. Andrews in Scotland. William initially studied art history, but changed to geography in his second year. Kate enrolled as an art history student. The two met during their first year of university and began dating in 2003.

■ While in Chile, William participated in a Raleigh International expedition, volunteering his time to work on community and environmental projects.

Being in university gave William a degree of **privacy**. The Royal Family had made an agreement with the **media** that William would be left alone while at St. Andrews. He could live a fairly normal life without worrying about having his daily activities detailed in newspapers and on television. This time allowed William and Kate to get to know each other.

By the time they graduated with their Master of Arts degrees in 2005, William and Kate were a couple. However, it was time for both to find a job. William began training to become a military officer. Kate was hired as a buyer for a clothing store chain. She also helped her parents run their party planning business.

■ When William graduated from St. Andrews on June 23, 2005, his father and stepmother, Camilla, came to support him.

Key Events

William and Kate continued their relationship after university. Kate could often be seen at events that William was attending. In some cases, she even attended events on his behalf. One such event was the marriage of William's cousin, Peter Phillips, in 2008. It was here that Kate met the queen for the first time.

Two years later, while on vacation in the African country of Kenya, William proposed to Kate. She accepted, and the two returned to England to make the formal announcement. On November 16, 2010, William and Kate told the world that they were engaged. Their wedding was to be held on April 29, 2011.

Excitement spread throughout the world. When the day arrived, people lined the streets of London in hopes of catching a glimpse of the bride and groom on their way to church. As each arrived at Westminster Abbey, the crowds cheered. Following the ceremony, William and Kate returned to Buckingham Palace to celebrate with friends and family. They left for their honeymoon the next day.

■ On William and Kate's wedding day, Queen Elizabeth II gave William the title of Duke of Cambridge. As William's wife, Kate became the Duchess of Cambridge.

Thoughts from William and Kate

William and Kate work hard to make an impact in the world. Here are some of their thoughts on life and being members of the Royal Family.

Kate discusses how important her family is to her.

"They've been great over the years—helping me with difficult times. We see a lot of each other and they are very, very dear to me."

Kate states her goals as a royal.

"...I hope I can make a difference, even in the smallest way. I am looking forward to helping as much as I can."

William talks about the way he wants to live his life.

"I think it's very important that you make your own decision about what you are. Therefore you're responsible for your actions, so you don't blame other people."

Kate talks about becoming a member of the Royal Family.

"It's obviously nerve-wracking, because I don't know the ropes really. William is obviously used to it, but I'm willing to learn quickly and work hard."

William discusses his future role as king.

"All these questions about do you want to be king? It's not a question of wanting to be, it's something I was born into and it's my duty."

William talks about choosing friends as a royal.

"I don't deliberately select my friends because of their background. If I enjoy someone's company, then that's all that counts."

What Is the Royal Family?

The United Kingdom has been ruled by royalty for centuries. Its first kings assumed leadership positions through war and politics. These kings ruled the land, making their beliefs the law. Over time, people became royal as a result of their family connections. The eldest son of a king, for instance, became king when his father died. Today, being royal is still connected to family and marriage.

Over the years, the United Kingdom's Royal Family has lost much of its political power. While the queen is the country's **head of state**, she does not make decisions on behalf of the country. Instead, the queen and her family act as **ambassadors** for the country. They attend events in the United Kingdom and around the world to show goodwill and promote tourism and industry. They also help organizations bring attention to social problems such as poverty and disease.

Today's Royal Family is made up of the queen and her husband, Prince Philip, and their children and grandchildren, along with several close cousins. Husbands and wives of these people are also considered to be part of the Royal Family. Members of the Royal Family all attend events on behalf of the queen and the country.

■ Members of the Royal Family often make appearances on the balcony of Buckingham Palace following important events, such as the Trooping the Color ceremony.

Royal Family 101

Queen Elizabeth (1926–)

Queen Elizabeth was born on April 21, 1926, to Prince Albert and his wife, Elizabeth. Prince Albert was only second in line to the **throne** of England. His brother, Edward, was meant to be king. However, Edward **abdicated** shortly after becoming king to marry a woman that the family did not approve of. As a result, Prince Albert became King George VI. When he died in 1952, his daughter Elizabeth became queen. Besides the United Kingdom, Elizabeth is also the head of state for Canada, Australia, New Zealand, and several island nations.

Prince Philip (1921–)

Prince Philip is Queen Elizabeth's husband. He is the son of Prince Andrew of Greece and Denmark, and Princess Alice of Battenberg. Philip was born in Corfu, Greece in 1921. However, his family was sent into **exile** the following year. Philip lived in France and Germany before settling in England. He married Elizabeth in 1947. In 1956, Philip founded the Duke of Edinburgh's Awards to encourage young people to have a sense of responsibility and be involved in their communities.

Prince Charles (1948–)

Prince Charles is the eldest son of Queen Elizabeth II and Prince Philip. He was born on November 14, 1948, at Buckingham Palace. Prince Charles was the first heir to the throne to attend regular school. Following graduation, he entered Cambridge University. He graduated with a Master of Arts in 1975. In 1981, he married Lady Diana Spencer, with whom he had two children, William and Harry. The marriage ended in divorce 15 years later. Charles married Camilla Parker Bowles in 2005. Prince Charles is known for his support of environmental causes.

Prince Harry (1984–)

Prince Harry was born in London on September 15, 1984. Following his regular schooling, he went to the Royal Military Academy at Sandhurst to train as an army officer. In 2007, he was deployed to Afghanistan to help the British war effort. Upon returning to England, he trained to become a military helicopter pilot and returned to Afghanistan in 2012. In his **civilian** life, Harry has represented the queen at several functions in various countries. He is also one of the founders of Sentebale, an organization that helps children suffering from HIV/AIDS in Africa.

Buckingham Palace

Buckingham Palace has been the official home of the British **monarch** since 1837. The palace has 775 rooms in total. Many of these rooms serve as offices for the royal staff. Other rooms contain priceless furniture and artwork. The queen holds ceremonies, dinners, and other events at the palace throughout the year. While these events are by invitation only, the general public is allowed to tour parts of Buckingham Palace in the summer months.

Influences

Prince William has had many people guide him throughout his life. As a future king, he has had several senior royals **mentor** him. Queen Elizabeth, in particular, has been advising William on his future role and helping him learn the responsibilities that come with being the ruler of several countries. Prince Phillip and Prince Charles have also provided William with the support he needs as he negotiates life as a royal.

When he was younger, William's mother wanted to make sure he had as normal a life as possible. Diana took William and Harry to amusement parks and fast food restaurants to give them an idea of how other children lived. She also wanted to make sure that they knew that there were other people in the world who did not grow up with the **privileges** that came with being royal. Diana made a point of taking her sons to homeless shelters so they could meet people who had a far more difficult life than they did.

■ William has great respect for his father and grandmother and the advice they give him. As future monarchs, both princes look to the queen as a role model.

Kate's family has been a steady support for Kate throughout her life. The family is very close. Kate and her sister are often seen having lunch together. William and Kate have even gone on vacations with Kate's family, including a 2013 holiday in the West Indies.

William and Kate's Family

In December 2012, William and Kate announced that they were expecting their first child. Prince George Alexander Louis was born on July 22, 2013. The family now lives in London's Kensington Palace.

■ Prince George was christened on October 23, 2013, at St. James's Palace in London.

Overcoming Obstacles

On August 31, 1997, Prince William's mother, Diana, was killed in a car accident in Paris, France. William was just 15 years old at the time. Even though he was in mourning for his mother, William still had royal duties. Along with other members of the Royal Family, William and his brother visited memorials set up to remember Diana and spoke with her fans. The two brothers also walked in her funeral procession along the streets of London.

Diana's death affected both boys deeply. They are determined to honor their mother's memory. Princes William and Harry have both taken up the charity work their mother once did. Each now serves as the **patron** for organizations to which Diana once lent her name. In honor of their mother, they organized a rock concert in London in 2007. All of the money earned at the concert was given to charity.

■ The *Concert for Diana* included performances by Elton John, Tom Jones, and Josh Groban. Held at Wembley Stadium, the event was attended by 60,000 people.

As a member of the Royal Family, William has always had to deal with the media. Following his mother's death, the attention increased. His time in university took him away from the media for a while. When he graduated, however, he was again the focus of **paparazzi** cameras. While William was used to the situation, he now had Kate to consider. She was not accustomed to this type of attention. William offered support and advice to Kate as she adjusted to the curiosity of the media and public alike.

Still, there are times when the media has overstepped its boundaries. When this has happened, Kate and William have issued statements to warn the media about possible legal action. In 2012, the couple took a French magazine to court when it printed pictures of Kate on vacation.

■ Although Kate often takes time to pose for photos, she also values her privacy. In 2013, William and Kate upgraded the security at their new home to protect their growing family from the paparazzi.

Achievements and Successes

Following their 2011 wedding, William and Kate embarked on their first official royal visit. The trip took them to the United States and Canada. Everywhere they went, crowds of people came out to greet them. The tour was a great success. The couple were soon invited to visit other countries as well. Tours to Malaysia, Singapore, Tuvalu, the Solomon Islands, and Denmark soon followed.

Even while assuming more royal duties, William has remained committed to his military career. He has made headlines around the world for his helicopter rescues of people in distress at sea and on land. In 2012, he was promoted from co-pilot to helicopter captain. This means he can now command operations in his own helicopter.

■ William is stationed at a Royal Air Force search and rescue base in Anglesey, Wales. He flies a Sea King helicopter.

In 2012, London hosted the Olympic Summer Games. William and Kate, along with Prince Harry, were named Olympic ambassadors. As the games approached, the three visited communities across the United Kingdom to promote the athletes and events. When the games started, they attended several events, both individually and together, to cheer on the British athletes.

HELPING OTHERS

In September 2009, Princes William and Harry started The Royal Foundation. Kate became a patron two years later. The charitable foundation provides funding for programs and causes of interest to the three royals. Currently, the foundation focuses on three main areas. It provides support to military personnel and their families, works with communities to protect the environment, and provides funding to youth programs so that young people can build confidence and achieve their goals.

Write a Biography

A person's life story can be the subject of a book. This kind of book is called a biography. Biographies describe the lives of remarkable people, such as those who have achieved great success or have done important things to help others. These people may be alive today, or they may have lived many years ago. Reading a biography can help you learn more about a remarkable person.

At school, you might be asked to write a biography. First, decide who you want to write about. You can choose a member of the royal family, such as William or Kate, or any other person. Then, find out if your library has any books about this person. Learn as much as you can about him or her. Write down the key events in this person's life. What was this person's childhood like? What has he or she accomplished? What are his or her goals? What makes this person special or unusual?

A concept web is a useful research tool. Read the questions in the following concept web. Answer the questions in your notebook. Your answers will help you write a biography.

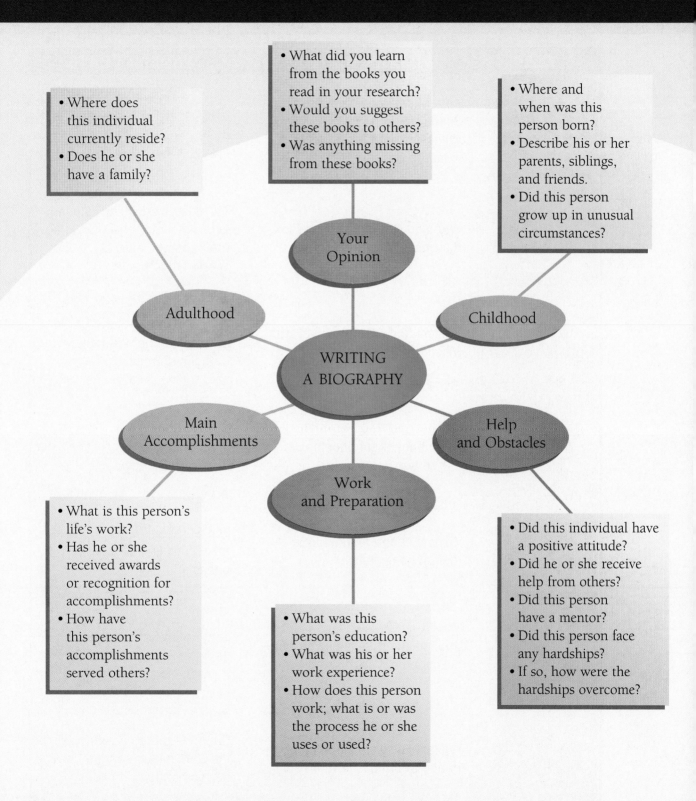

- Where does this individual currently reside?
- Does he or she have a family?

- What did you learn from the books you read in your research?
- Would you suggest these books to others?
- Was anything missing from these books?

- Where and when was this person born?
- Describe his or her parents, siblings, and friends.
- Did this person grow up in unusual circumstances?

Your Opinion

Adulthood

Childhood

WRITING A BIOGRAPHY

Main Accomplishments

Help and Obstacles

Work and Preparation

- What is this person's life's work?
- Has he or she received awards or recognition for accomplishments?
- How have this person's accomplishments served others?

- What was this person's education?
- What was his or her work experience?
- How does this person work; what is or was the process he or she uses or used?

- Did this individual have a positive attitude?
- Did he or she receive help from others?
- Did this person have a mentor?
- Did this person face any hardships?
- If so, how were the hardships overcome?

Timeline

YEAR	WILLIAM AND KATE	WORLD EVENTS
1982	Kate Middleton is born on January 9, in Reading, England. William is born on June 21, in London.	Great Britain and Argentina go to war over the Falkland Islands.
2001	Kate and William start classes at the University of St. Andrews.	Terrorists attack key locations in the United States, including the Pentagon and New York's World Trade Center.
2005	William and Kate graduate with Master of Arts degrees.	Cardinal Joseph Ratzinger is elected Pope of the Roman Catholic Church.
2009	William and Harry form The Royal Foundation. Kate becomes a patron two years later.	Barack Obama is inaugurated for his first term as U.S. president.
2010	William and Kate announce their engagement.	The Burj Khalifa, the world's tallest building, officially opens in Dubai.
2011	William and Kate marry on April 29, in London's Westminster Abbey.	The United States formally declares an end to the war in Iraq.
2013	William and Kate's first child, Prince George, is born on July 22.	Queen Elizabeth celebrates the 60th anniversary of her coronation.

Key Words

abdicated: gave up power

ambassadors: people who act as representatives

civilian: a person not in the armed forces

democracy: a government that is elected by the people of a country

exile: sent away from a country

gap year: a break taken by a student before continuing further studies

head of state: the person who holds the highest position in a country's government

heir: a person who is to receive the money, property, or position of a person after that person has died

media: sources of news and information, such as newspapers, television, and magazines

mentor: to advise or train someone

monarch: a person who rules over a kingdom or empire

paparazzi: a photographer who pursues celebrities to get a picture of them

patron: a person, especially one who is rich or powerful, who supports or helps another person, a group, or a cause

privacy: the condition of not being observed or disturbed by other people

privileges: special rights given to a person or group

throne: the power or authority of a king or queen; the chair that a king or queen sits in during special ceremonies

United Kingdom: a country in western Europe consisting of England, Scotland, Wales, and Northern Ireland

volunteer: a person who offers to help or does something by choice and often without pay

Index

Log on to www.av2books.com

AV² by Weigl brings you media enhanced books that support active learning. Go to www.av2books.com, and enter the special code found on page 2 of this book. You will gain access to enriched and enhanced content that supplements and complements this book. Content includes video, audio, weblinks, quizzes, a slide show, and activities.

AV² Online Navigation

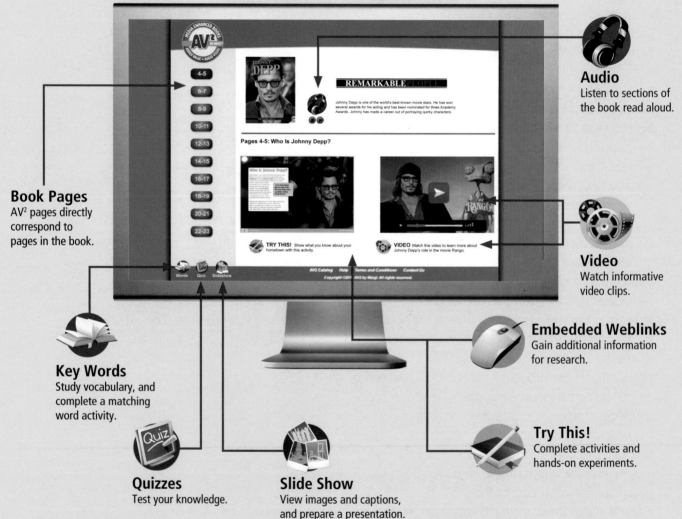

Book Pages
AV² pages directly correspond to pages in the book.

Audio
Listen to sections of the book read aloud.

Video
Watch informative video clips.

Key Words
Study vocabulary, and complete a matching word activity.

Embedded Weblinks
Gain additional information for research.

Try This!
Complete activities and hands-on experiments.

Quizzes
Test your knowledge.

Slide Show
View images and captions, and prepare a presentation.

AV² was built to bridge the gap between print and digital. We encourage you to tell us what you like and what you want to see in the future.

Sign up to be an AV² Ambassador at www.av2books.com/ambassador.